They that hope in the Lord will renew their strength, they will soar as with eagles' wings; They will run and not grow weary, walk and not grow faint.
Isaiah 40:31

**The intent and
purpose of this volume is to
give you faith, hope and
inspiration. Hopefully it will help bring
peace and tranquility into your life. May
it be a reminder of God's love, guidance
and His many blessings.**

**Our publications help to support our work
for needy children in over 130 countries
around the world. Through our
programs, thousands of children are
fed, clothed, educated, sheltered
and given the opportunity to
live decent lives.**

Salesian Missions wishes to extend special thanks and gratitude to ou generous poet friends and to the publishers who have given us permission to reprir material included in this book. Every effort has been made to give prope acknowledgments. Any omissions or errors are deeply regretted, and the publisher, upo notification, will be pleased to make the necessary corrections in subsequent editions.

Cover photo: ©kc31958/iStockphoto.com

First Edition Printed in the U.S.A. by Concord Litho Group, Concord, NH 03301.

A Beacon of Hope

from the
Salesian Collection

Compiled and Edited
by Jennifer Grimaldi

Illustrated by
Russell Bushée, Paul Scully,
Frank Massa, Robert VanSteinburg,
Maureen McCarthy, Gail L. Pepin,
Bob Pantelone, Dale Begley,
and Dorian Lee Remine

Contents

Christ Is Life 6

He Exists 7

Butterflies Are Free 8

I'm Sending You
   Some Flowers 11

By Faith..................................12

Share God's Gifts 14

The Grandest Gift 15

Let's Thank God 17

The Hills and the Trees 19

Ask of Him 20

I Have a Talk With Jesus 21

He Lives 22

Peace....................................24

Count Your Blessings 25

Trying Times of Life 27

The Power of Our Prayer 28

Enjoy Everyday 30

All 31

Dancing Leaves 32

His Word................................34

Giving 35

The King's Highway 37

Farewell to Winter 39

Renewing Hope 40

Praise to God 41

God Can Make Things
   Right Again 42

Learning to Trust 44

Song of My Soul 46

Spring Is Here 47

His Guidance 49

When Spring..........................50

He Will Lead Your Way 51

There's Something About
   a Garden............................52

Oh, Gracious Lord… 55

Don't Pass Me By...................56

Come With Me 57

Treasures of Our Lord 58

The Best Thing You Can Do 60

He Gives You Strength 61

God Makes Everything Right....62

God Is Love 65

Each Bright Tomorrow 67

Faith to Move That Mountain....68

When the Load Gets Heavy 70

I Owe It All to You 71

Master Artist 72

A Gift for God.........................74

Come to Me All Who
    Are Weary...........................77

When I Think of Winter 78

Keep in Touch With Jesus 80

A Touch of Spring 81

Yesterday, Today,
    and Tomorrow 82

The Windows of Life 84

A Gentle Reminder 87

The Hills Sing of You.............88

A Precious Time 90

Awareness...............................91

The Special Season 92

Bequest...................................95

Trusting...................................96

Eternal Love...........................97

Just a Tiny Mustard Seed 98

Within My Soul 100

Summer Day..........................101

To Offer Thanks 102

God's Garden 104

At Dawning...........................105

Behold, He Knocks Today!....106

Meeting.................................108

Time With a Friend Is
    Time Well Spent 109

The Sunshine of
    Your Love 110

Prayer for Guidance.............111

He Leadeth Me... 112

The Road Ahead 114

There Is Peace in the Storm....115

Autumn's Beautiful Array 116

Friends 118

God Is There.........................119

Rely on the Lord 121

When Troubles Come 122

The Learner 124

Look Forward 125

Born Again 126

Well Done, My
    Beloved Child 128

Christ Is Life

Christ stills the raging waters
When fears and troubles rise,
And when the path is darkened,
He's still our stay, our guide.

He's the bread come down from Heaven,
He's the water in life's well;
He's the very joy of living
For He is life, itself.

Loise Pinkerton Fritz

He Exists

God exists no matter what men may say –
He unfolds the lovely flowers in Spring,
Autumn yields her harvest bountifully,
And in Summer the robins sing!

A rosebud blooms with such perfection –
Definitely an act of God;
While a tiny crocus emerges
Out of the frozen sod.

Never believe that God isn't around
Especially when Winter's chill is near;
For He guides the geese in V-formation
Knowing safely just where to steer.

'Tis true the seasons come and go
And time just doesn't stand still,
But our heavenly Father, He's always around
While we journey each valley and hill!

Linda C. Grazulis

*But these are written that you
may come to believe that Jesus is
the Messiah, the Son of God,
and that through this belief you
may have life in His name.*
John 20:31

Butterflies Are Free

Butterflies are free,
So are the sun's warm rays,
And breezes that refresh us
On Summer's humid days.

Free is fresh air we breath
All through the day and night;
The lovely flowers that bloom,
Arrayed in colors bright.

And all of Nature's glory
Are free for all to see;
The mountains, hills, and starry skies,
The mighty ocean's seas.

The flowers that spread their fragrances,
Perfumes that Nature made,
The tall majestic trees
That spread their welcome shade.

Smiles have no price, they're free
To spread their cheer around,
Reflecting God's great love
And His blessings that abound.

Helen Gleason

My strength and my courage is the Lord, and He has been my Savior. He is my God, I praise Him; the God of my Father, I extol Him.
Exodus 15:2

I'm Sending You Some Flowers

I'm sending you some flowers –
Not the ordinary kind.
These will not wither or fade,
For they come from God divine.
A sweet bouquet of kindness
With some tender buds of home,
And faith's colorful blossoms,
To give you the strength to cope.
All these surrounded with
The beautiful fragrance of love,
Arranged just for you from God's
Heavenly garden above.

Steven Michael Schumacher

*Charm and beauty delight
the eye, but better than
either, the flowers of the field.*
Sirach 40:22

11

By Faith

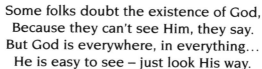

Some folks doubt the existence of God,
Because they can't see Him, they say.
But God is everywhere, in everything…
He is easy to see – just look His way.

I see Him in the tiniest flower,
I feel Him in the morning breeze.
How can we affirm His presence?
Just witness the beauty of stately trees.

The mighty oceans surge to and fro,
Majestic mountains reach for the sky,
The beauty of a happy child...
The existence of God I cannot deny.

I touch His softness in a delicate rose,
A snowflake is His unique design.
He shares with the eagle His Majesty...
The fragrance of a lilac – He made divine.

I hear Him in the bluebird's song,
I sense His peace in my daily prayer.
He abides in the comfort of a mother's love...
I just know He is always there.

Charles Clevenger

*Whatever you ask for in prayer with
faith, you will receive.*
Matthew 21:22

Share God's Gifts

Take the time, caress a rose,
God's gifts are everywhere,
Blossoms on your pathway
Tell you He is near.

Listen well to angels' songs,
Their whispers gently call,
Fill your heart with Charity –
Care when brothers fall.

Extend a loving hand of Hope,
Share this earthen space,
For Faith will gather us again
In God's eternal grace.

Carol MacAllister

Let's Thank God

To be able to view a sky of blue
And the green of earth below;
A sunrise gleaming with purple and red
And the colors of sunset's afterglow...

Let's thank God for the wonders He wrought;
That He, too, declared were good,
Then, for our benefit He lovingly brought...
Let's thank and praise Him, as we should.

Don't take for granted all the things God made,
Like Winter's snow and Summer's shade...
Flowers that bloom in early Spring,
Songs the robins cheerfully sing...

All these from God's own precious hands,
His treasures with pleasure, He gave our lands...
Be mindful to thank Him every day...
Lest all these wonders be taken away.

Lou Ella Cullipher

*Sing to the Lord, all the
earth, announce His
salvation, day after day.*
1 Chronicles 16:23

For God commands the angels to guard you in all your ways. Psalm 91:11

The Hills and the Trees

The hills move in a circle
All around the valleys low
Like a scalloped edge of greenness –
A panoramic show.

Amassed with trees in Summer,
They guard the lands below;
And keep them green and silent
Until the wild winds blow.

The trees that reach the highest
Sweep the heavens with their leaves –
Caressing blue sky's softness;
Singing with each breeze.

The hills and trees of majesty
Live through every storm.
May nothing end their beauty,
Nor disturb their quiet form.

Joan Stephen

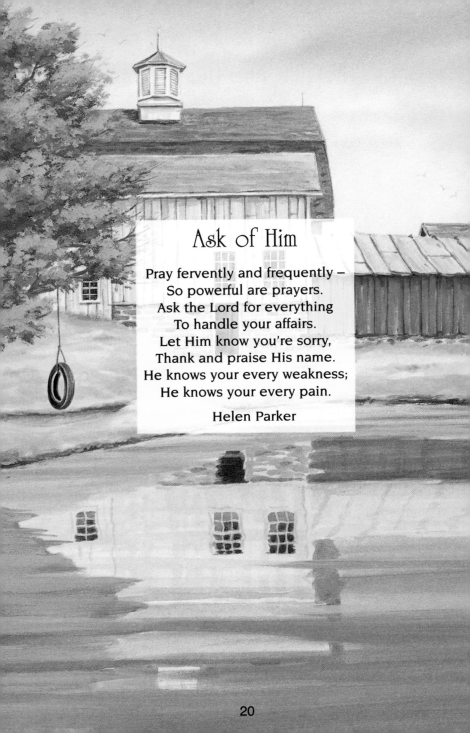

Ask of Him

Pray fervently and frequently –
So powerful are prayers.
Ask the Lord for everything
To handle your affairs.
Let Him know you're sorry,
Thank and praise His name.
He knows your every weakness;
He knows your every pain.

Helen Parker

I Have a Talk With Jesus

I have a talk with Jesus
When things are going wrong.
And He will always listen –
To Jesus I belong.

He knows all things about me;
My needs He does fulfill.
I trust in what He tells me –
He says "Peace! Peace – be still."

For, He's my Lord and Savior;
Our Father's precious Son.
And He will solve all problems –
Yes! Every single one.

His peace is always with me;
He is my guiding Light.
So, I have a talk with Jesus –
And all things turn out right.

Edna Massimilla

He Lives

I see Him in the sunset
With its muted crimson glow,
The crowning of a lovely day
As oceans ebb and flow.
Not only in the mountains
Can His Majesty be seen,
But in a tiny leaf of gold
Of a spreading chestnut tree.

In fields of yellow buttercups
Or crimson-petaled rose,
In every plant and flower bloomed
I see His love exposed.
And in small rivulets
That flow o'er rocks and hills,
To mighty oceans' rolling tides
With foaming waves He fills.

His love has made a world for us
If we would only see,
The treasures of the Universe
And all of it is free.
I stand in awe and worship before
His wonders grand displayed,
And praise the mighty One whose
Worlds with miracles arrayed.

Helen Gleason

Do you not know or have you not heard?
The Lord is the eternal God, creator of the ends
of the earth. He does not faint nor grow weary,
and His knowledge is beyond scrutiny.
Isaiah 40:28

23

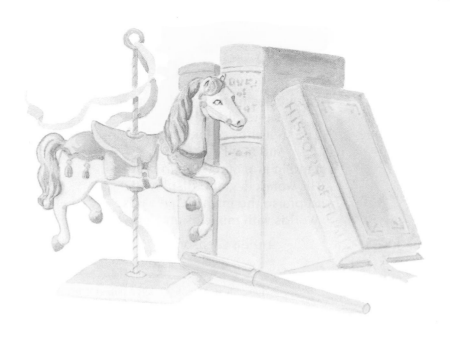

Peace

My home is never empty, although I be alone,
I hear the voices of angels,
To God their love intone!
I feel His very presence
In wind and storm or rain
That beats upon my window and quiets all my pain!
I see His face in every nook,
Each cranny of my room;
I know He's ever near to me
To chase away my "secret gloom."
I'm sure He'll never leave me,
His promise He'll fulfill –
To keep me close, in home and heart,
And softly whisper, "Peace – Be Still."

Kathryn Wiesenhoefer

Count Your Blessings

Count your blessings, one by one;
Thank God for every gift.
Reach out to those who are in need,
And give someone a lift...

Count your blessings, one by one;
The Lord is by your side,
And He will fill your coffers full,
Whatever may betide...

Count your blessings, one by one;
Remember God is love,
And He will touch your heart with peace,
And guide you from above...

Count your blessings, one by one;
Rejoice and praise the Lord,
And He will hold you in His hand,
And give you just reward!

Hope C. Oberhelman

The Lord by wisdom
founded the earth,
established the heavens
by understanding.
Proverbs 3:19

Trying Times of Life

During the trying times of life
When hardship comes your way,
Just call upon your Savior,
Then go to Him and pray.

Always let your heart be open
And listen to what He shares;
Never doubt His words of wisdom
For it is He who really cares.

Remember tomorrow is another day
And peace and joy follows strife;
Hold steadfast to your faith in God
During the trying times of life.

Shirley Hile Powell

*The child grew and
became strong, filled with
wisdom; and the favor of
God was upon him.*
Luke 2:40

27

The Power of Our Prayer

There comes a time in each one's life
When heartaches will prevail.
Our efforts to control them all
May often fall and fail.

We can cope with daily problems,
Mundane things we can resolve;
Yet, overwhelming trials may come
That God alone can solve.

When faith, undaunted, magnifies
In thought, in word, in prayer,
He hears our pleas and answers them,
Embraced in loving care.

God does respond to all our needs
With promises of peace,
To lift our hearts and to redeem
His love that will not cease.

Implicit trust and confidence
Are blessed bonds to share,
Transcended by almighty God
Through the power of our prayer.

Patience Allison Hartbauer

*You listen, Lord, to the needs of
the poor; You encourage them
and hear their prayers.*
Psalm 10:17

Enjoy Everyday

Enjoy everyday that's been given
And life will be sweeter by far,
No matter the place or the moment –
God loves you wherever you are.

Enjoy everyday; it's a treasure.
There is nothing on earth could compare
To the sunrise of morn in its beauty,
And a quiet tranquil moment of prayer.

Katherine Smith Matheney

All

There's been so many, many times, Lord,
I've felt alone and blue,
Calling out to You, my Friend,
To show me what to do.

I trust in Your every word,
I know each one is true.
I know I can depend on You
To guide and see me through.

There never is a day, Lord,
That I am not in need
And when I call, I know You're there
Taking care of all indeed.

Dona M. Maroney

*Guide me in Your truth and teach
me, for You are God my Savior.
For You I wait all the long day,
because of Your goodness, Lord.*
Psalm 25:5

Dancing Leaves

When the wind blows, the leaves dance
To music we can't hear
As if the trees were whispering
That Winter's very near.
Leaves swing and sway and pirouette
And take their final bow
Returning to their Mother Earth
To be reborn somehow.
They create a lovely picture
In colors bright and gay
When Autumn reveals her grandeur
Before she slips away.

They fascinate and enchant us
In their gowns of red and gold.
When they waltz in Nature's ballroom,
It's a sight to behold!
Too soon the landscape fades to brown
Etched with evergreen,
But soon the scene will change again
For snowflakes have been seen.
Autumn waltzes by on angel wings,
Curtsies and takes a bow
Then leaves us all the memories
That Heaven will allow!

Clay Harrison

His Word

There in His Word I find comfort,
There in the depth of His prayers,
There in the promises given,
Is respite from worries and cares.

There in my darkness is sunlight,
There in my turmoil is peace,
And there in my sorrow is joy,
When my fears and concerns I release.

These burdens I daily would carry,
I'm reminded to give to the Lord,
As He tells me with love never ceasing,
To believe and to trust in His Word.

Judith B. Schwab

Giving

I wish I were a rich man;
I would help each day,
Others in this needy world –
So much I'd give away.

To bring a smile to a saddened face
With just a wink, a word,
To do the things that God has taught
To show Him I have heard.

Take a tear from a weeping eye,
Comfort... all about;
This is our legend here in life
No one should be without.

I once met a wise man here
And this is what I heard him say:
"The more you give of yourself in life,
The more you take away."

James Joseph Huesgen

*God's way is unerring; the Lord's
promise is tried and true; He is a
shield for all who trust in Him.*
Psalm 18:31

35

The King's Highway

Let's walk upon the King's highway
As through this life we fare;
Here God's patrolling day and night,
He'll keep us in His care.
When storms arise, He'll shelter us
And hold us close to Him;
He is the Light of this old world,
No day can e'er be dim.

While walking on the King's highway,
Turn neither left nor right;
Just keep your eyes on Jesus, friend,
He'll keep you in the light.
And when, at last, Heaven's gate we reach,
Each step will be worthwhile,
For we'll see Jesus face to face;
He'll welcome home His child.

Loise Pinkerton Fritz

*Have mercy on me, God, have
mercy on me. In You I seek shelter.
In the shadow of Your wings I seek
shelter till harm pass by.*
Psalm 57:2

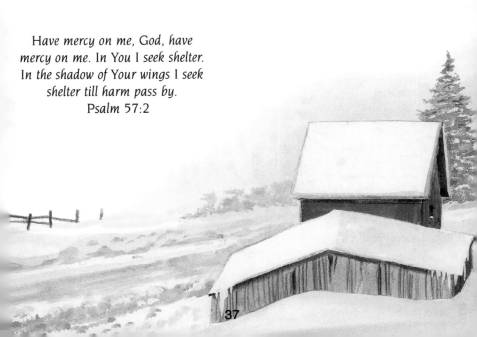

I *have heard that the spirit of God is in you, that you possess brilliant knowledge and extraordinary wisdom.*
Daniel 5:14

Farewell to Winter

The Winter will not stay,
The Winter will go by,
Gone will be the silver snow
And purple, pewter sky.

No more the subtle colors of
The dormant, restless dune.
The Winter will not stay
For Spring will be here soon.

Welcome to the verdant buds
That brighten every tree,
Welcome to the turquoise sky
So brilliant on the sea.

How good to feel the sun's golden rays
Fall strong upon one's face.
How good to see white blossoms
Falling down like lace.

Spring comes to our island,
God's land along the sea;
Windswept wonder whistling by
So bright, so wild, so free!

Marybeth Greenhalgh

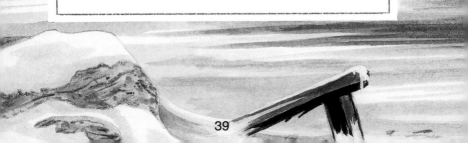

Renewing Hope

What ails your heart, that you are sad
And filled with heaviness?
What fear has caused these trembling hands –
This painful weariness?

Is not the God, the Mighty One,
The King upon His throne?
Will He abandon those He loves
To struggle on their own?

His heart is love, His hand is strong –
His purpose will prevail.
If you believe, obey and trust,
Your faith need never fail.

Anita G. Hamill

Praise to God

How great to be a child of God,
How wonderful each day!
How comforting is the peace He brings
To us along the way!

Oh, how I love and praise God's name
For all He's done for me,
And how I pray His tender care
Will ever, always be.

Alone, I could not bear my load
Of daily stress and woe,
But in God's ever-loving arms,
I'm safe where e'er I go.

May His love forever enfold me
Wherever I may roam,
And when my days on earth are over,
May He gently lead me Home.

Mary S. Chevalier

*I give You thanks, O God of my
Father; I praise You, O God my
Savior! I will make known Your
name, refuge of my life;*
Sirach 51:1

41

God Can Make Things Right Again

God can make things right again
When everything goes wrong,
He can mend a broken heart
And fill it with a song.

Then He can take the grey skies
And turn them all to blue,
And even hang a rainbow
To show how He loves you.

Should you go to bed at night
And find you cannot sleep,
Just talk to the Good Shepherd,
Be still and don't count sheep.

Yes, trust in Him completely
And hold fast to His hand,
He knows your every heartache;
He cares and understands.

He is a loving Father,
He cares for His own,
He's someone you can count on –
You need not feel alone.

God can mend a broken heart,
Thus fill it with a song;
Somehow make things right again
When everything goes wrong.

Mary E. Herrington

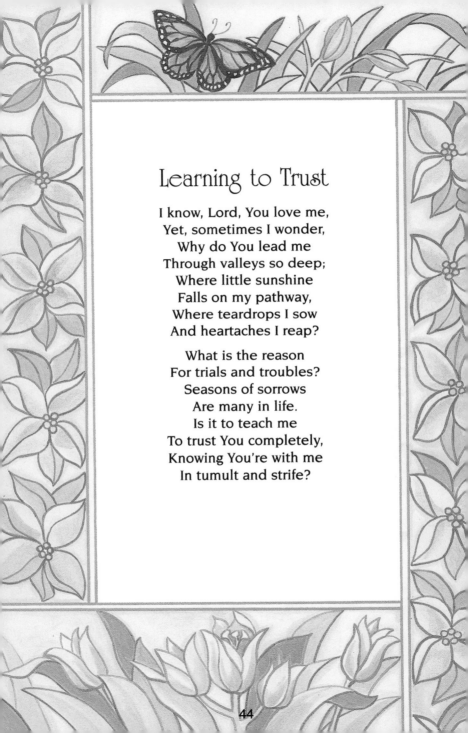

Learning to Trust

I know, Lord, You love me,
Yet, sometimes I wonder,
Why do You lead me
Through valleys so deep;
Where little sunshine
Falls on my pathway,
Where teardrops I sow
And heartaches I reap?

What is the reason
For trials and troubles?
Seasons of sorrows
Are many in life.
Is it to teach me
To trust You completely,
Knowing You're with me
In tumult and strife?

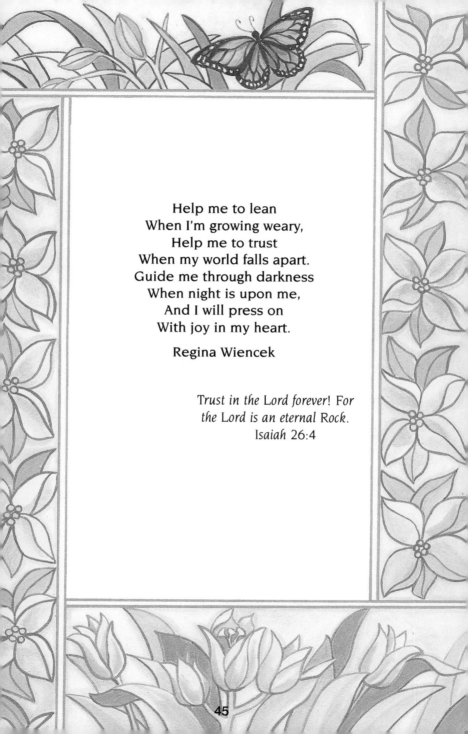

Help me to lean
When I'm growing weary,
Help me to trust
When my world falls apart.
Guide me through darkness
When night is upon me,
And I will press on
With joy in my heart.

Regina Wiencek

*Trust in the Lord forever! For
the Lord is an eternal Rock.*
Isaiah 26:4

Song of My Soul

The song of my soul
Is a hymn of praise
To my Lord, Jesus,
I sing every day,
Whether it's raining,
Or the sun shines bright,
Throughout carefree days,
Or long, troubled nights;
The song of my soul
Shall forever be
A lovesong to God,
My heart's melody.

Steven Michael Schumacher

Spring Is Here

Oh, what beauty now beholds me!
Spring adorned her very best.
The frozen earth now melted
Tells me Winter is now at rest.

Green grass blankets the earth
While flowers appear everywhere.
Farmers are plowing fresh sod
After Winter left it bare.

The springtime air is fresh and crisp
And the sun is warm and bright.
The sky is of azure blue
Until the stars dazzle in the night.

May the Spring bring happiness to you
As it is the season that I like best.
Everything is alive and thriving
And has survived Winter's test.

Shirley Hile Powell

*Adorn yourself with grandeur and
majesty, and array yourself with
glory and splendor.*
Job 40:10

47

You need endurance to do
the will of God and receive
what He has promised.
Hebrews 10:36

His Guidance

Release the urge to struggle,
Just turn it over to Him.
Things will then unfold for you;
With Him you'll always win!
Let your consciousness expand
To life's full, wider vision;
Releasing expectations,
He will join in your decisions.
Ask for guidance and step forth
And let Him lead the way.
Enjoy the journey with your Guide!
From Him you'll never stray!

Ruthmarie Brooks Silver

When Spring

When yellow tulips open up
Resembling sunshine in a cup;
When flowers blossom endlessly
And fill my eyes with pageantry...

When every grassy knoll is green,
When leaves upon the trees are seen;
When birds are winging fancy-free,
When Winter is in absentee...

When the days are April-dressed
Bringing mayflowers on request;
When thunder-clouds sail into view –
That's when I'll know springtime is due.

Nora M. Bozeman

He Will Lead Your Way

Are you feeling blue?
Stressful day and night?
Put your trust in Jesus…
Things will turn out right!

Do not doubt or fear,
Bow your head and pray.
Jesus solves all problems…
He will lead your way.

As you greet the morn,
Sunshine will appear.
Thank the Lord for blessings…
Things will then be clear.

Faith shall make you whole;
You'll have a happy day.
Jesus solves all problems…
He will lead your way.

Edna Massimilla

*As the rising sun is clear to
all, so the glory of the Lord
fills all His works.*
Sirach 42:16

There's Something About a Garden

There's something about a garden
That sets your mind at ease
As you inhale the fresh air
And feel the cooling breeze.
There is beauty to delight you
Everywhere you look,
And small creatures may surprise you
In every cranny and nook.

There's something about a garden
That changes day by day,
For something new is growing where
Something old has gone away.
There are veggies, herbs or flowers
Each season of the year,
Some that you have planted there
And some that volunteer.

There's something about a garden
That turns our thoughts to God,
For every seed is a miracle
Growing beneath the sod.
A garden's never finished for,
We only see in part
The ever changing masterpiece
Of Nature's finest art.

Clay Harrison

Oh, Gracious Lord...

Oh, gracious Lord and Savior,
We give our hearts to Thee;
We need Thy everlasting love
To set our spirits free.

Oh, gracious Lord and Savior,
We kneel to Thee in prayer;
We raise to Thee our voices, Lord,
For Thou art ever there.

Oh, gracious Lord and Savior,
Remember us, we pray,
For we are lost and lonely, Lord,
And we need Thee all the way.

Oh, gracious Lord and Savior,
Come hold us in Thy hand,
And teach us what we need to know
That we may understand!

Hope C. Oberhelman

Don't Pass Me By

Don't pass me by my Jesus,
My soul must not be lost.
My heart must be unfettered,
No spirit tempest tossed.
Stay at my side, my Jesus,
Please guide me on my way.
Throughout the narrow passage
Protect me from the fray.

Marilyn McNeil de Latour

Come With Me

Come with me, we'll roam the fields,
In the bright, warm Summer sun,
And chase the laughing seagulls
On the beach there as we run.
Please come with me, and we'll climb
The rocky mountain so high,
Then try to count diamond stars,
Sparkling in the midnight sky.
Our great God has made this world;
What beautiful sights to see!
I long so much to share them...
My dear, will you come with me?

Steven Michael Schumacher

*You have made known to
me the paths of life; You
will fill me with joy in
Your presence.*
Acts 2:28

Treasures of Our Lord

Footprints in the sand of life
Are quickly washed away,
As the ebb and flow of time
Recedes from shore each day.

And those who walk life's sandy shore
Know it's a swift repast,
For nothing that is gathered here
Will truly ever last.

For all creation turns to dust
And we pass from this earth –
Memories are all we leave
From the moment of our birth.

Leaving words wrapped, bright, in love,
Sharing faith with friends,
Are valued gifts that we bequeath
To commemorate our end.

Our legacy comes not from gold
Or what humankind's adored,
It's giving of yourself in love
As treasures of our Lord.

Nancy Watson Dodrill

The Best Thing You Can Do

When someone has a problem,
The best thing you can do,
Is to be right there beside them;
They need someone like you.

You don't have to say a word,
Or state your point of view.
You'll help more if you listen;
The best thing you can do.

Ruth Moyer Gilmour

He Gives You Strength

The God of Heaven gives you strength,
As you journey on life's road.
You may think, "I'm not so strong,"
As you carry your life's load.

But, by God's grace, He sends to you
Help along the way.
A caring neighbor, a faithful friend,
Or someone just to pray.

We are all God's family,
So we never are alone.
We bear each other's burdens.
Until He takes us Home.

Mary Ann Jameson

The Lord's love for us is strong;
the Lord is faithful forever.
Hallelujah!
Psalm 117:2

God Makes Everything Right

Never give up in time of trials
For soon they will fade away.
God will hold us close to Him
And is with us night and day.

When our hearts are heavily burdened
And our minds are filled with fear,
It's then we fail to remember
That our God is always near.

He never leaves His lost lambs
No matter how far we wander.
He gently pulls us back to Him
And it is then we begin to ponder.

Though our hearts are heavy
And we try to close the door
On the One who truly loves us
And wants to help us all the more…

Let us give Him our woes and worries
As He understands our plight
And never fail to remember
It is God who makes everything right.

Shirley Hile Powell

Beloved, let us love one another, because love is of God; everyone who loves is begotten by God and knows God. Whoever is without love does not know God, for God is love.
1 John 4:7,8

God Is Love

How sweet the name of Jesus
To every listening ear;
It calms the restless spirit
And dries the flowing tear.

It cures the deepest heartache,
Restores joy to the heart;
It sheds a ray of mercy
To all, both near and far.

It's a transforming power
That comes from Heaven above,
And it bears yet another name,
The One we know as Love.

Loise Pinkerton Fritz

*Restore my joy in Your
salvation; sustain in me
a willing spirit.*
Psalm 51:14

But I believe I shall enjoy
the Lord's goodness in
the land of the living.
Psalm 27:13

Each Bright Tomorrow

When I greet the day each morning,
Though the rain is on its way,
I see the bright tomorrow
That I asked for yesterday.

For I have so many blessings
That the rain can't wash away;
So I start right in enjoying
What I asked for yesterday.

With the boundless hope and promise
I find inside my cottage door,
I just go on with my living –
Couldn't ask for any more.

Don't understand why folks are lonely
When there's so much to be done.
Though the clouds are hanging heavy,
Just look past them to the sun.

When the storm clouds all pass over
And the sun is on its way,
We all can greet the bright tomorrow
That we asked for yesterday.

Gertrude Blau Byram

*Let my prayer come before
You; rescue me according
to Your promise.*
Psalm 119:170

Faith to Move That Mountain

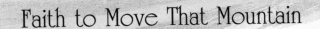

When the hills are difficult to climb
And the valleys seem cave deep,
Let us soar on the mighty wings of faith,
O'er the hills and valleys leap.

Faith is the evidence; though, we don't see,
A gentle breeze on a windy day;
Gales of laughter permeating the air,
A strew of merry hearts along life's way.

A fluttering sparrow that flies the nest –
No solid ground beneath its feet,
Or a seed that's planted 'neath the sod
Yielding forth golden grains of wheat.

So hold onto faith and only believe,
For an acorn grows a towering tree.
God has the answer, the reprieve –
A way to set a captive, troubled soul free.

A wee bud that unfolds a beautiful rose,
Drying our tears with heartfelt prayer,
Trusting in God though problems surround –
Casting on Him our every care.

Linda C. Grazulis

*Faith is the realization of
what is hoped for and
evidence of things not seen.*
Hebrews 11:1

When the Load Gets Heavy

When the load gets heavy and you feel despair,
Call on the Lord who's always there.
He's right by your side each hour of the day
To make your load lighter along the way.

Sometimes the road is bumpy and rough.
He knows your endurance, when you've had enough.
He gives you strength to overcome all
And He may let you stumble, but never fall.

Helen Parker

Rejoice in hope, endure in affliction,
persevere in prayer.
Romans 12:12

I Owe It All to You

There are dark days ahead,
Bright and joyful ones, too.
No matter what the day may bring,
You always see me through.

You guide me on my merry way;
You lighten my heavy load.
No matter which way I go
You're on that very road.

God, I lift my hands to You
In eternal praise.
I'll sing to You forever
As my grateful voice I raise.

Dona M. Maroney

*It is good to give thanks to
the Lord, to sing praise to
Your name, Most High.*
Psalm 92:2

Master Artist

God is the ultimate artist,
Color and form – He knows.
To confirm His artistic talents,
Look closely at the heart of a rose.

He knows how to apply the colors,
His brushstrokes – subtle or bold;
He paints the sky a heavenly blue,
The trees of Autumn – burnished with gold.

He sets the evening sky ablaze
On a canvas of crimson and gold;
The awesome beauty of His artistry –
Is a visual treat to behold.

He dapples the sky with fleecy clouds
And scatters them about with the breeze.
Stars add sparkle to a black night sky
Like diamonds on a celestial frieze.

He paints the Winter with ice and snow
To cover the drab and gloom.
He splashes His palette with cleansing rain,
Bringing springtime alive with bloom.

He brings life and soul to His masterpiece
With the beauty of birds on the wing.
The meadows flow with graceful rhythm...
I clearly hear the landscape sing.

Yes, God is the consummate artist,
With brushstrokes that speak to my heart.
I stand in awe at the beauty
Of His masterful works of art.

Charles Clevenger

A Gift for God

He doesn't need a present
All wrapped and tied with a bow;
Nor words of adoration,
Without good deeds to show.
But there's one thing He'd like from you
That no one else can give:
A gift to surely honor Him,
As long as you shall live.

That gift is you! You're quite unique:
A presence on this earth!
And how you choose to live your life
Determines that gift's worth!
Be of service to the Lord!
Make your goodness known!
You're bound to make a difference,
For we reap what we have sown.
Be a candle where you live
And help to light the way.
Make your corner of the world
Shine brighter, every day!

Carol Barron-Karajohn

Come to me, all you who labor and are burdened, and I will give you rest.
Matthew 11:28

Come to Me All Who Are Weary

The night is dark, the room is cold;
There's sadness everywhere.
But Someone hears and Someone cares
To lift your dark despair.
Sit silently and listen,
Feel His presence in the air.
Turn to Him with all your longings,
Tell Him all your cares.
Remember that He promised
He would help you every day.
Give Him your heavy burdens;
Let Him show the way.
The night will change from darkness,
The room will warm with love
The moment that we give our lives
To our heavenly Father above.

Mary Ann Carter Houston

May the Lord, the God of
your fathers, increase you a
thousand times over, and bless
you as He promised!
Deuteronomy 1:11

When I Think of Winter

When I think of Winter
I start to shiver so –
As I recall those snowflakes
And the winds that harshly blow.
The trees seem, oh, so barren
For the leaves have tiptoed away –
I long for Autumn colors
And for a sunny Summer's day.
When I think of Winter
I also see snowmen being born
And ponder why I feel such loss –
Oh, so empty and forlorn.

There were younger years I used my sled
And created angels in the snow,
Took a hike whistling in those furry boots
And spotted a white-tailed doe.
Days of happiness amid the cold –
My spirit spared with glee,
Praising God for Winter's reign
And for the wonders I did see.
When I think of Winter now
I'll try and be thankful it has arrived.
With memories I'll gather warmth –
Truly it's great to be alive!

Linda C. Grazulis

Keep in Touch With Jesus

Keep in touch with Jesus
Each hour of the day –
Jesus, the Lord and Savior,
Who washed our sins away.

On the Cross at Calvary
He took our guilt and shame.
Jesus, Lord and Savior,
All praises to His name.

In the realms of glory
He listens to our prayer –
Jesus, Lord and Savior,
Who keeps us in His care.

Trust Him and obey Him
All morning, noon and night.
Keep in touch with Jesus,
Our precious, guiding light!

Edna Massimilla

For God who said, "Let light shine out of
darkness," has shone in our hearts to
bring to light the knowledge of the glory
of God on the face of Jesus Christ.
2 Corinthians 4:6

A Touch of Spring

Just when our eyes grow weary
Of Winter's ice and snow,
God sends a touch of springtime
To set our hearts aglow.

The little brook is gurgling,
So happy to be free;
The robin's in the tree again
Singing new melodies.

The grass is sprouting green
Where lately snowflakes lay;
The crocus is pushing through
Along the garden way.

The sky is turning brighter blue,
The Winter's on the wing,
And I am, oh, so happy
With just a touch of Spring.

Kay Hoffman

*Beside them the birds of
Heaven nest; among the
branches they sing.*
Psalm 104:12

Yesterday, Today, and Tomorrow

My mind goes back to yesterday,
To fond memories I hold dear,
A time of youth and innocence,
Stored up year after year.
The happiness of childhood days,
With loving friends I knew,
Joys of family get-togethers,
As we dreamed, loved, and grew.
The family is now scattered,
Many friends have moved away.
Some loved ones have departed,
Life is not the same today.

Today I have grown older,
Have a family of my own.
I have seen tears and sorrow,
But my heart has bigger grown.
I have hopes of a bright tomorrow,
And a future without fear;
For I have someone to share it,
My God whom I hold dear.
He helps me with my problems,
Lifts me up by wings of love,
And when earthly life is finished,
He will take me Home above.

Frances Culp Wolfe

The Windows of Life

The windows of life are open,
Each with a different view
Of city lights and country roads,
Perhaps a detour or two.
Sometimes our windows need cleaning
When we're unable to see
New opportunities before us
Waiting there patiently.
The windows of life are portals
That open wide each day,
Allowing us to come and go
To places far away.

We can see the things before us
And things we leave behind,
While we chart a course less traveled
And say what's on our mind.
We live and die by choices we make,
So it's important to know
Where we're going and where we've been
Each time we pack to go.
Sometimes we don't see the "big picture"
But only see in part
'Til God draws back the curtains
Revealing His works of art!

Clay Harrison

Answer me, Lord, in Your
generous love; in Your great
mercy turn to me.
Psalm 69:17

A Gentle Reminder

A gentle tongue brings healing,
So let your words be kind.
Words can mend a broken heart
And sooth a troubled mind.

Stoop down and lift the fallen,
In love extend your hands.
The erring soul needs mercy,
Someone who understands.

A true friend in all seasons
Is like a treasured gift,
Nearby in times of trouble
And helps your burden lift.

Regina Wiencek

*Finally, brothers, rejoice. Mend your
ways, encourage one another, agree with
one another, live in peace, and the God
of love and peace will be with you.*
2 Corinthians 13:11

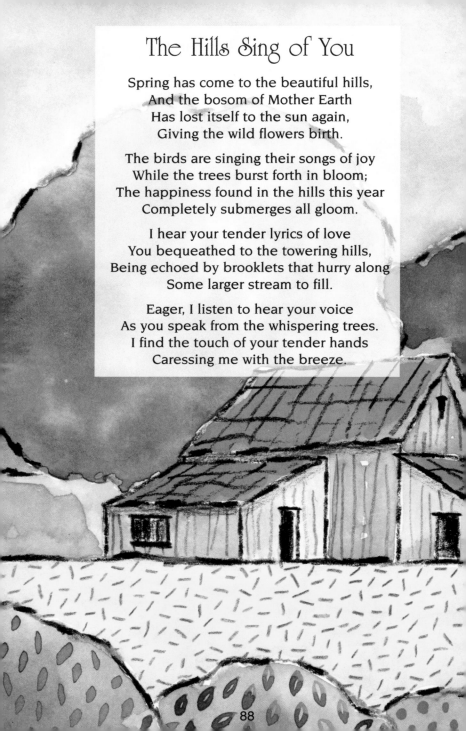

The Hills Sing of You

Spring has come to the beautiful hills,
And the bosom of Mother Earth
Has lost itself to the sun again,
Giving the wild flowers birth.

The birds are singing their songs of joy
While the trees burst forth in bloom;
The happiness found in the hills this year
Completely submerges all gloom.

I hear your tender lyrics of love
You bequeathed to the towering hills,
Being echoed by brooklets that hurry along
Some larger stream to fill.

Eager, I listen to hear your voice
As you speak from the whispering trees.
I find the touch of your tender hands
Caressing me with the breeze.

Then anxious to see your face again,
I climb from the brook below,
To the path that leads to our favorite spot:
It's the way that we used to go.

Then I see you! I see you! My eyes are filled
With tears of joy untold,
As you smile at me from each opened flower
With that same sweet smile of old.

Spring has returned to the beautiful hills,
With splendor… shining and new;
More wonderful… precious, than ever before.
Yes, this year, the hills sing of you.

Anna Lee Edwards McAlpin

A Precious Time

We need a precious time of prayer
Before a loving God to kneel;
It may not be on bended knee,
Our heart reveals the way we feel.

A precious time to tell our Lord
The inner secrets of our heart;
We cast each burden at His feet,
Our every care will then depart.

Oh, thank You, Lord, for loving us –
We often fail but still You care;
We thank You for amazing grace
And for a precious time of prayer.

Gertrude B. McClain

*How precious is Your love,
O God! We take refuge in
the shadow of Your wings.*
Psalm 36:8

Awareness

Lord, make me aware of each blessing –
The ones that I miss every day,
Like skies that are blue and flowers in bloom,
And friends that I meet on my way.

When my negative thoughts are too many,
And only the dark clouds I see,
Remind me, oh Lord, of Your presence,
In this day You have given to me.

Even when stillness surrounds me,
And thoughts are the company I keep,
Let Your word and Your spirit be with me,
Bringing comfort and peace to my sleep.

And tomorrow when cares would confront me,
I will take a few moments to rest,
To look at the sky and the flowers,
And think of the ways I am blessed.

Judith B. Schwab

The Special Season

Spring heralds now
Her gentle show
With bluebell spill,
Where once "grew" snow.

Lilies in their valley scent
Spring breathes, a fragrant focus,
Scatters pastel tinted buds
Of dainty, dancing crocus.

Sweet violets hide shyly near
In shadowed pasture spaces,
While apple trees rejoice the breeze
With petaled pink embraces.

"All come, all come," Spring says
From russet-colored throat.
Behold the sacred promise kept,
As gratefully we note.

His resurrection traced,
Redrawn with Nature's hand;
Life renewed and lasting
Through the glory of the Lamb.

Bea Lotz

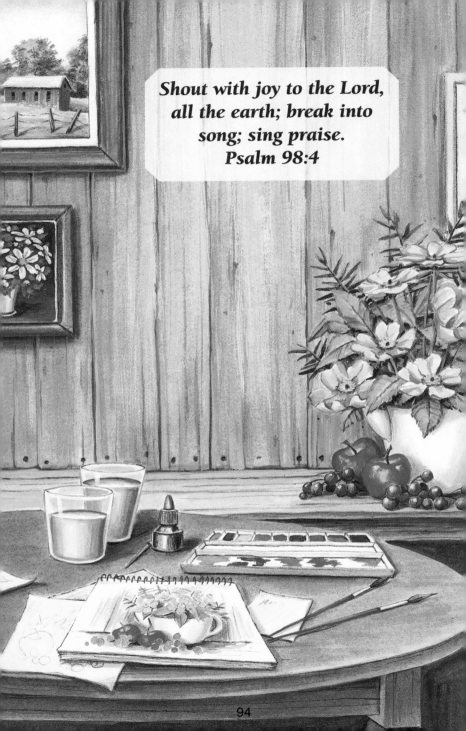

Shout with joy to the Lord,
all the earth; break into
song; sing praise.
Psalm 98:4

Bequest

If I can write one song to leave the world,
And if that song can cheer a lonely heart;
If I can write one poem to lift some soul
Above their deep despair, and hope impart;

If I can paint some scene of loveliness,
A touch of beauty which would linger on,
To bless the world, and add a bit of grace
To lives long after I have lived and gone;

If I can plant somewhere a seed of love
To later blossom into a happy smile,
Or do a kindly act to ease one's pain,
I'll know my living then has been worthwhile.

And though I leave no jewels or wealth behind,
It matters not for they cannot compare
To treasures of the heart... the gift of self
Which I bequeath the world with love to share.

Beverly J. Anderson

*Moreover, God is able to make
every grace abundant for you, so
that in all things, always having
all you need, you may have an
abundance for every good work.*
2 Corinthians 9:8

95

Trusting

Because we trust in God's care and protection,
We know He'll lead us in the right direction...
Leading us on by His guiding light
Should we stumble and fall in the darkest night;
Compassion for us in our deepest sorrow,
Trusting He'll bring a glad tomorrow.
Let us praise and thank Him more each day,
While trusting He'll bring us through life's stormy way.

Because we trust in God's truth and grace,
We should always wear a smiling face...
Never feeling "all down in the dumps,"
Trusting He'll get us "over the humps"...
Smoothing the way as we walk close to Him,
Lighting the way when the shadows grow dim...
Leading us on to that beautiful shore
Where we'll live and trust Him forevermore!

Lou Ella Cullipher

Eternal Love

I walk along a shimmering beach,
Leaving footprints in the sand.
'Tho all alone, I walk with faith
That my Lord will hold my hand.

Seagulls float on the updraft breeze
With effortless strength and power.
God's Love is like that every day...
No matter the plight, the place or the hour.

I pause to watch the incessant surf
Crash gently on the pristine shore.
Eternal is this awesome power...
God's love – is even more.

Charles Clevenger

Just a Tiny Mustard Seed

Just a tiny mustard seed –
So insignificant and small,
Is the size of faith you'll need
When to God you humbly call.

Yes, all things are possible
If only you believe,
And God will not refuse you,
According to His will you can receive.

Faith can lift and shift a mountain,
Only trust God's love and care –
Hold onto hope and patience,
View an eagle soaring in the air.

For miracles surround us –
Why should we fret and stew
When God created the universe
And those skies of azure blue?

Just a tiny mustard seed –
Much smaller than a pea,
Will cause our doubts to dwindle
When we use eyes of faith to see.

Linda C. Grazulis

Within My Soul

Lord, I feel special within my soul;
I feel so honored and I feel whole.
My Jesus loves me the way I am –
He is the Master and I His lamb.

I praise my Savior; He's good to me…
He gave His life once to set us free.
He suffered surely and paid the cost
So that our souls all would not be lost.

When storm clouds gather, He sends the sun
Shining down from Heaven on everyone.
He is our Shepherd, He guards His sheep
Always and ever within His keep.

Lord, I am thankful each night I pray
My sins forever are washed away.
Within my soul, Lord, I'm feeling free –
I love my Jesus; He's good to me.

Katherine Smith Matheney

Summer Day

I was looking from my window
On a lovely Summer day.
The sky was filled with beauty
As the sun gave off its ray.

It seemed the sky just split wide open
With light shining from above.
It seemed I saw straight into Heaven
As God was sending down His love.

God had blessed me with His beauty
On that special Summer day,
And I knew that He had planned it
Just for me in His own way.

So, I give God all the glory
For allowing me to see
The sky and all its beauty
He had sent down just for me.

Bonnie J. Knapp Lyons

*May we shout for joy at your
victory, raise the banners in the
name of our God. The Lord
grant your every prayer!*
Psalm 20:6

To Offer Thanks

We need to offer thanks to God
For all He does each day.
He sends so many blessings
To brighten up our way.

He blesses us with loving friends
Who fill our hearts with cheer;
And daily He supplies our needs
So we never have to fear.

We cannot even fathom
The fullness of His love,
The mercy and forgiveness
From His storehouse up above.

He guides us on life's journey
Through each peril that's ahead.
And with His hands to lead us,
There is nothing we should dread.

So don't forget to thank Him
For His constant loving care.
Give Him praise and adoration
As you seek His will in prayer.

Frances Culp Wolfe

You are my God, I give You
thanks; my God, I offer You praise.
Psalm 118:28

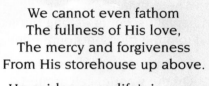

God's Garden

In quiet, restful solitude
Where time is standing still –
A fragrant scent is wafting through
From the blossoms on the hill.

A time to sit and meditate
On the wonders all around –
To find a heart of gratitude
For the blessings that abound.

A thankful heart can bring the joy
Of flowers blooming near
And words of praise before our God
Can wash away the fear.

God's garden is the place to be,
If only in my heart.
His peace is waiting there for me,
His love will not part.

Anita G. Hamill

At Dawning

Another dawn is breaking
As I wake to face the day.
I know my Lord will hear me
In the prayers I convey.

I seek His precious wisdom,
Plead for His mighty power,
To give me strength and courage
Through every blessed hour.

I behold the glow of sun rays,
Heaven's light comes shining through,
God's majesty reflecting
Onto all things that I view.

I'm uplifted and encouraged
By God's glorious display.
I trust that He anoints me
At the dawning of this day.

Patience Allison Hartbauer

*At dawn may the Lord bestow
faithful love that I may sing
praise through the night,
praise to the God of my life.*
Psalm 42:9

105

Behold, He Knocks Today!

Today He stands and gently knocks
Upon your heart's door, friend.
He's waited patiently before
And each time you'd pretend
You did not hear, felt such could wait,
Perhaps some other day;
A self-willed path you chose instead
And turned the Lord away.

Again, He stands and gently knocks.
Will you invite Him in?
He'll change your life, forgive your sins,
And give you peace within.
He'll be your Savior and your friend,
No one could love you more;
So trust the Lord to save your soul,
In faith unlatch the door.

He promises Eternal Life
To all who will believe.
What will your answer be, my friend,
Will you the Lord receive?
Come to Him now without delay,
Time's fleeting day by day;
Tomorrow might not come at all,
Behold, He knocks today!

Beverly J. Anderson

*For everyone who asks, receives; and the
one who seeks, finds; and to the one who
knocks, the door will be opened.*
Matthew 7:8

Meeting

In the silence of God's presence,
I rejoice, kneel and pray,
Giving thanks for safekeeping,
And for strength another day.

His provision ever constant,
His presence ever sweet,
His mercy, grace, abounding,
His love, so full, complete.

Norma Woodbridge

*I will delight and rejoice in
You; I will sing hymns to
Your name, Most High.*
Psalm 9:3

Time With a Friend Is Time Well Spent

It's time well spent when you enjoy
A couple of laughs and tea for two –
Recalling nostalgia, the good ole days
Over a perking kettle of brew.

It's time well spent sharing
In word, deed, or thought,
Seconds and minutes and hours –
Treasures which can't be bought.

It's time well spent smiling,
Adding cheer is close to one's heart –
Even if someone is distant
You still can be friendly apart.

It's time well spent to be friendly –
Create a relationship that is loving, honest, true;
And like a boomerang you'll soon discover
That friendship has flown back to you!

Linda C. Grazulis

*Light dawns for the
just; gladness, for the
honest of heart.*
Psalm 97:11

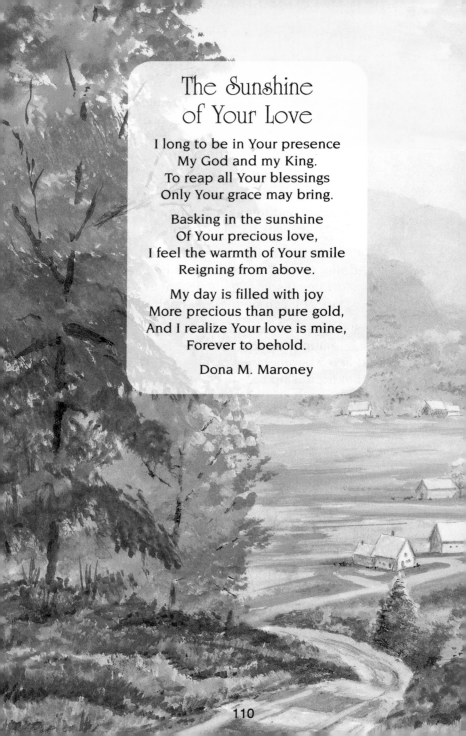

The Sunshine of Your Love

I long to be in Your presence
My God and my King.
To reap all Your blessings
Only Your grace may bring.

Basking in the sunshine
Of Your precious love,
I feel the warmth of Your smile
Reigning from above.

My day is filled with joy
More precious than pure gold,
And I realize Your love is mine,
Forever to behold.

Dona M. Maroney

Prayer for Guidance

Give me wisdom, God, I pray,
To wisely use the hours today,
To fill them with some special deeds
And let me sow some Christian seeds.

Help this pilgrim on the way,
Hear me as I bow to pray.
Flood my thoughts with victory,
Listen to my heartfelt plea.

Guide my footsteps everyone
As morning starts, 'til day is done.
Forgive my failures and renew
My yearning for the good and true.

And if I falter in my quest,
I know with love You still will bless.
So give me wisdom, God, I pray,
To wisely use the hours today.

Virginia Borman Grimmer

*Teach me to do Your will, for You
are my God. May Your kind spirit
guide me on ground that is level.*
Psalm 143:10

He Leadeth Me...

The Lord is my salvation,
The rock on which I stand,
My friend and my companion
Who takes me by the hand.

He leads me to the mountaintop
And through the valleys low,
And bids me rest beside still waters
When I am faint to go.

He sees my many faults and yet
He never does condemn,
But gently nudges me once more
To come and follow Him.

He is my beacon on the hill,
The lamp unto my feet;
He is the staff on which I lean
When hills of life are steep.

When I'm hungry for His word
He prepares a feast for me,
And opens wide His sacred text
That I more clearly see.

No matter what the future holds,
Whatever it may be,
I will not fear the path ahead
The dear Lord leadeth me.

Kay Hoffman

The Road Ahead

As we grow older and bodies weaker,
We need not fear the road ahead.
Never alone as we journey onward
When faith replaces pangs of dread.

Today is the day that each is given;
There will be showers of blessings for you.
God wants you to share with friends you meet
That your source of joy may become theirs too.

We have seen the beauty of His creation
With its new birth day after day.
Bumps we endure make the smooth places sweeter
As we near the end of the way.

Sing songs of praise while you have a voice,
Give thanks for the gifts you receive.
Pray for peace in hearts that are troubled;
God gives to all who believe.

M. Elaine Fowser

There Is Peace in the Storm

Let troubles come and pressures mount,
God's ways are always best.
A lesson is concealed within
Each problem, every test.

Let darkness fall and storm clouds rise,
Wild winds sweep o'er my soul;
In every gale He gives sweet peace,
A calm, when billows roll.

Darkness must flee before the light,
And trials and troubles cease.
Content I'm waiting for the morn,
My heart in perfect peace.

Regina Wiencek

*May the Lord give might to His
people; may the Lord bless His
people with peace!*
Psalm 29:11

Autumn's Beautiful Array

Here it is again, dear Lord,
The autumntime of the year,
When the earth is flaming with color
And the nights are chilled and clear.

The frost is scattered lightly
Over the crisp and dampened grass.
The beauty is overwhelming.
How I wish it all could last.

Autumn once again reveals
Its treasures of reds and gold.
No other season is more daring,
As everywhere brilliance explodes.

Silver streaks across the meadow
Shimmer in stalks of ripened corn,
And provide an awesome wonder
Made by spiders in the early morn.

I know this spectacular splendor
Must one day fade away,
But memories will surely linger
Of Autumn's beautiful array.

Shirley Hile Powell

*O Lord, our Lord, how awesome is Your
name through all the earth! You have
set Your majesty above the heavens!*
Psalm 8:2

Friends

Friends really are the frosting
On the cake of life;
They love us on our good days
Or in times of strife.

They always are so ready
To lend a helping hand,
And if we are troubled
They're sure to understand.

Having friends is wondrous;
They enrich us everyday,
And help to lessen burdens
As we travel on our way.

So, I give thanks for friendships,
The old ones and the new,
For they are of great value
And to them I am most true.

Virginia Borman Grimmer

God Is There

In the dark times of my life
I wonder if God cares.
I question my faith and hope
For the trials are difficult to bear.

I often question my commitment
When my spirits are very low;
I wonder if this will be
The end – the final blow.

No matter what my struggle,
No matter how great the pain,
He is always there beside me,
For ever-present is His name.

He is the Great Almighty
Who knows me through and through,
And with this understanding
I'll do the best that I can do.

Barbara Joan Million

Rely on the mighty Lord;
constantly seek His face.
Psalm 105:4

Rely on the Lord

I must rely on You, Lord,
In everything that I do,
For I know with absolute certainty
That Your words are trustworthy and true.

My trust in You must not falter
As my strength is drawn from You.
You give me the power and courage
To conquer each day anew.

To live my life for You, Lord,
Is to keep You in my heart
And make You the Master of my soul,
Knowing that You will never depart.

Let all that is within me
Give You praise and glory each day,
And may I never fail to give thanks
For the happiness sent my way.

Shirley Hile Powell

*God indeed is my Savior; I am
confident and unafraid. My
strength and my courage is the
Lord, and He has been my Savior.*
Isaiah 12:2

When Troubles Come

When sorrows overwhelm you
And bring you to your knees,
It can truly test your faith
In troubled times like these.
When the road is filled with detours
And potholes everywhere,
There's nowhere to find comfort
But in the arms of prayer.
Troubles sadly come in bunches
And knock us off our feet,
And every minor victory
Is often bittersweet.

They say joy comes in the morning
If we survive the night,
And some tears will surely flow
Before we see the light.
We can wallow in self-pity
Or stand our ground and fight,
For God helps those who help themselves
And sorrows will take flight.
With faith there is always hope,
And hope brings victory
To those who place their trust in Him
For all the world to see.

Clay Harrison

The Learner

A quiet heart of gratitude,
A gentle heart of prayer,
A tender heart of love and grace,
To comfort and to cheer.

A loving heart of faithfulness,
A servant's heart to bless,
A humble heart of thanks and praise,
God's mercies to confess.

Norma Woodbridge

Look Forward

Do not be discouraged
When clouds obscure your view,
They all too soon will fade away
And let the sun shine through.

As day does always follow night
And night does follow day,
You'll find your apprehensions
Will also fade away.

Yesterday has long since gone,
Tomorrow's far away,
So live your life unto the full
While there is still today.

Harold F. Mohn

*For you were once darkness, but
now you are light in the Lord.
Live as children of light.
Ephesians 5:8*

Born Again

Things seemed unimportant as
I searched for happiness:
I found success and yet it could not
Fill this emptiness.

Today I gave my life to Him.
My sins He washed away;
In righteousness and dignity
I'll follow in His way.

I'll walk the path of glory 'neath
The shelter of His wing,
And when He calls me home,
I'll hear the hallelujahs ring!

Rejoice! Rejoice! For I am whole,
With joy He's filled my heart;
I revel in this burning love,
From which I'll not depart.

Let's sing out loud, and raise our hands
As we praise His Holy Name,
For now that I am born again –
I shall never be the same.

Angie Monnens

Glory in His Holy Name; rejoice,
O hearts that seek the Lord!
1 Chronicles 16:10

Well Done, My Beloved Child

My mistakes have been many;
My sins in great store,
But Jesus paid my penalty;
Washed me white forever.
And I feel so tired and weary
Because often do I fall.
So long is my life's journey
But I heard my Master's call:
He said to always love others –
To do good along life's way,
And to trust my Lord and Savior
Each and every day.
When I'm finished with my journey,
I long to hear God say:
"My beloved, precious child – well done,"
And, "Welcome home, today."

Barbara A. Lott